Why We Need WATER

Constance Lundberg

REAL LIFE readers™

Rosen Classroom™

New York

Water is all around us.

It is in oceans and rivers.

Clouds are made of water.

Rain is water that falls

from clouds.

People have water at home.

They need water to clean.

People need water to drink.

Water helps keep people healthy.

Plants need water to grow.

Water helps keep plants healthy.

Plants need water to live.

They die without water.

They become brown and dry.

Animals need water to drink.

They use it to wash, too.

Fish need water to swim.

They could not live without water.

Why do you need water?

Why We Need WATER

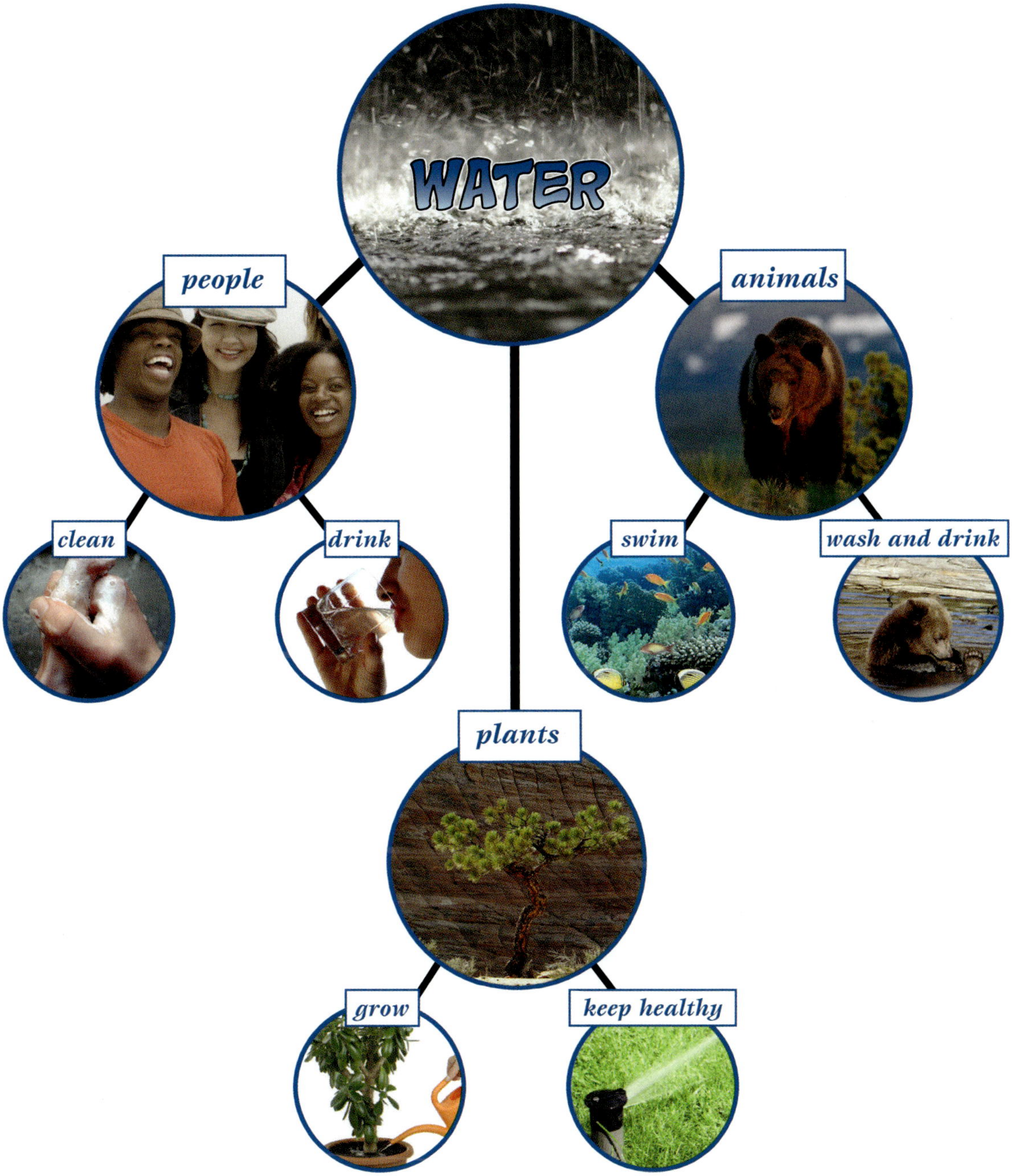

WORDS to KNOW

clouds

ocean

rain

river

water

Praise for *ImagiNation*

Like an autograph from a childhood hero, the book should trigger happy memories for all children of Toronto television.

— Richard Crouse, film critic

As someone who grew up watching oodles of TV as a kid in the 1960s and 1970s, and then as a television host watched by a generation of young Canadians in the 1980s and 1990s, I've experienced how television leaves indelible marks on young hearts and minds. Ed Conroy's well-researched book, *ImagiNation*, took me down memory lane, sharing behind-the-scenes stories about the shows that coloured my world when I was a kid, when television was everything, and I believed everything was possible.

— Erica Ehm, former MuchMusic VJ

A much-needed compendium of the history of Canadian television. Coming from an era where we threw out tapes regularly, I'm thankful for Ed and Retrontario for creating such a rich archive for us to enjoy.

— Phil Guerrero (a.k.a. PJ "Phresh/Fresh" Phil),
former host of YTV's The Zone

Ed Conroy … has lovingly produced the definitive history of kids' TV programs to date.… For this book, through his love of the genre and extensive research, he has unearthed numerous kids' TV shows, many of which are deeply etched in the hearts and souls of our inner child.… So if you're like me, and you believe that children's programming is important to our culture, or if you're just feeling downright nostalgic, read this wonderful book!

— Nina Keogh, TV history consultant and puppeteer

ImagiNation is full of sumptuous detail, important history, and honours the people who created those programs. For me, it was *The Friendly Giant*, *Mr. Dressup*, *Razzle Dazzle*, and *The Forest Rangers*. For you, it will be a half-dozen other amazing programs. Lucky for us, Canada was particularly good at making kids' shows. And lucky for us, Ed has gathered them all up and preserved them in this book. It truly is a tickle trunk of wonder.

— Terry O'Reilly, host of CBC's *Under the Influence*

I don't know anyone who cares more and has done more to preserve the history of children's television in Canada than Ed Conroy. And I don't know where we'd be without him.... He does it because he cares about preserving the legacy of so many talented people, who have created so many wonderful memories through time.

— Steve Paikin, former host of TVO's *The Agenda*

Ed Conroy is a preeminent cultural historian, archivist, and vintage video sleuth.

— Moses Znaimer, co-founder of CityTV